MUSIC NOTATION G

The Grand Staff

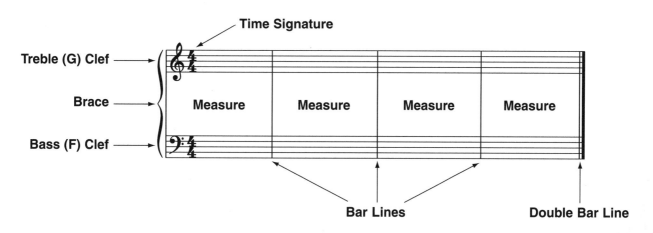

Time Signatures

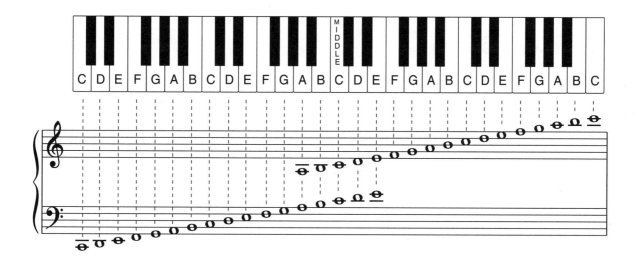

2 = 2 beats in each measure
4 a **quarter note** gets one beat

3 = 3 beats in each measure
4 a **quarter note** gets one beat

4 = 4 beats in each measure
4 a **quarter note** gets one beat

Notes

Eighths	Quarter	Dotted Quarter – Eighth	Half	Dotted Half	Whole

Rests

Eighth	Quarter	Half	Whole

Stems and Beams

Notes **below** the middle line are written with stems up.
Notes **on** or **above** the middle line are written with stems down.

The stem direction of beamed notes or chords is determined by the note farthest from the middle line.

Accidentals

 A **sharp** sign before a note means to play the next key to the right, either black or white.

 A **flat** sign before a note means to play the next key to the left, either black or white.

 A **natural** sign cancels a sharp or flat. Play the *natural* (white) key.

Tempo Marks

Tempo marks tell the speed of a piece, and often its character or mood.

Adagio = Slowly, seriously

Andante = Walking speed, calmly

Andantino = A slightly faster tempo than *Andante*

Allegro = Quickly, happily

Dynamic Signs

Dynamic signs tell how loudly or softly to play, and help create the mood of the music.

pp *(pianissimo)*	very soft
p *(piano)*	soft
mp *(mezzo piano)*	medium soft
mf *(mezzo forte)*	medium loud
f *(forte)*	loud
ff *(fortissimo)*	very loud
◁ *(crescendo)*	gradually louder
▷ *(decrescendo)*	gradually softer

Musical Terms

slur (*legato* touch)   play smoothly and connected

staccato   play short and separated

tie   play the first note and hold through the next

accent   play the note louder

Musical Terms (continued)

8va	*8va* - - - - - - - - - ¬	play one octave higher than written
	8va _ _ _ _ _ _ _ _ _ ⌋ *8vb* _ _ _ _ _ _ _ _ _ ⌋	play one octave lower than written
15ma	*15ma* - - - - - - - - ¬	play two octaves higher than written
loco		play the notes where written (after playing 8va or 15ma)
ritardando (rit., ritard.)		slow the tempo gradually
a tempo		return to the original tempo
repeat sign	:‖	return to the beginning or the nearest ‖: and play again
D.C. (Da Capo) al Fine		return to the beginning *(Da Capo)* and play until you reach the sign for the end *(Fine)*
D.S. (Dal Segno) al Fine		return to 𝄋 *(segno)* and play to the end *(Fine)*
D.C. al Coda		return to the beginning and play to the first coda sign ⊕ ; then skip to the next coda sign ⊕ and play to the end